YOUNG SCIENTIST CONCEPTS & PROJECTS

CAMERAS

CHRIS OXLADE

Gareth Stevens Publishing
MILWAUKEE

The original publishers would like to thank the following pupils from Hampden Gurney School: Gary Cooper, Diane Cuffe, Sheree Cunningham-Kelly, Louisa El-Jonsafi, Sarah Ann Kenna, Lee Knight, Shadae Lawrence, Robert Nunez, Kim Peterson, Paul Snow and Kisanet Tesfay. They would also like to thank Keith Johnson and Pelling Ltd. for the loan of props and Nikon UK Ltd. and Intel Corporation UK for the loan of pictures.

Gareth Stevens Publishing would like to thank Jon Allyn, Master of Photography, Photographic Craftsman for his assistance with the accuracy of the text. Mr. Allyn, the 1997 Wisconsin Photographer of the Year, has earned over 300 local, state, and national awards.

For a free color catalog describing Gareth Stevens' list of high-quality books and multimedia programs, call 1-800-542-2595 (USA) or 1-800-461-9120 (Canada). Gareth Stevens Publishing's Fax: (414) 225-0377. See our catalog, too, on the World Wide Web: http://gsinc.com

Library of Congress Cataloging-in-Publication Data

Oxlade, Chris.
Cameras / by Chris Oxlade.
p. cm. — (Young scientist concepts and projects)
Includes bibliographical references and index.
Summary: Describes what is inside a camera, how it works, and how to use it. Includes simple experiments and projects, such as how to make your own camera, as well as tips on taking better photographs.
ISBN 0-8368-2085-1 (lib. bdg.)
1. Photography—Juvenile literature. 2. Photography—Study and teaching (Elementary)—Activity programs—Juvenile literature. 3. Cameras—Juvenile literature. [1. Cameras.] I. Title. II. Series.
TR149.O94 1998
771—dc21 97-41626

This North American edition first published in 1998 by
Gareth Stevens Publishing
1555 North RiverCenter Drive, Suite 201
Milwaukee, WI 53212 USA

Original edition © 1997 by Anness Publishing Limited. First published in 1997 by Lorenz Books, an imprint of Anness Publishing Inc., New York, New York. This U.S. edition © 1998 by Gareth Stevens, Inc. Additional end matter © 1998 by Gareth Stevens, Inc.

Managing Editor, Children's Books: Sue Grabham
Editor: Ann Kay
Consultant: Peter Mellett
Photographer: John Freeman
Stylist: Marion Elliott
Designer: Caroline Reeves
Picture Researcher: Marion Elliott
Illustrators: Richard Hawke, Caroline Reeves
Gareth Stevens series editor: Dorothy L. Gibbs
Editorial assistant: Diane Laska

Printed in the United States of America

1 2 3 4 5 6 7 8 9 02 01 00 99 98

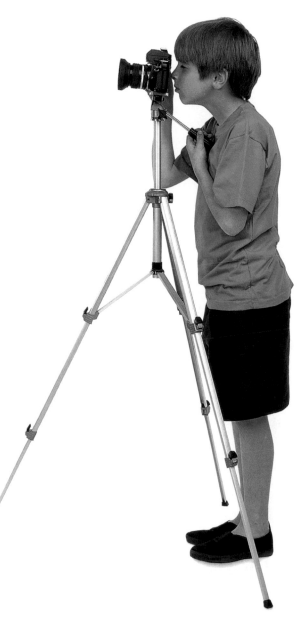

CAMERAS

CONTENTS

YOU AND YOUR CAMERA

WHAT is the one vital piece of equipment you must not forget when you take a vacation? Your camera! To most people, a camera is simply a device for taking snapshots of places, people, animals, etc. But cameras also are sophisticated machines that make use of the latest breakthroughs in science and technology. A camera is designed to do a specific job – to make a copy of a scene on film by collecting light from that scene and turning it into a picture. It works in a way very similar to your eyes, but it makes a record of the scene instead of simply seeing it.

Open and shut
Using a camera is like looking through a special window. Open and close your eyes very quickly. This is how a camera records light from a scene.

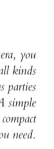

With your camera, you can record all kinds of events, such as parties and vacations. A simple point-and-shoot compact camera is all you need.

Early cameras
The first practical cameras with film were developed in the 1830s. Today, cameras do the same job, but they are much easier to use. In the early days, it could take as long as half an hour to take a photo, and the photographer had to stand under a large hood.

4

Producing prints

A camera is worthless without film to record images (a digital camera uses a microchip instead of film). If you want prints, the film is developed, or processed, and negatives are produced. Prints are made from the negatives. Which of the negatives on this strip *(right)* produced the print next to it?

Negative   *Print*

Getting it right

When professional photographers are shooting sports or news events, they must capture the event clearly. Their pictures appear in magazines and newspapers to enhance the story.

Professionals at work

Professional photographers usually use very sophisticated equipment to get the best results. They probably carry two or three cameras, a selection of different lenses, and dozens of rolls of film.

WHAT IS A CAMERA?

ALL cameras, from disposable to professional models, have the same basic parts. The camera body is really just a lightproof box that keeps the light-sensitive film in complete darkness. The film is held flat in the back of the camera body. The lens is at the front of the body. It collects light from the scene and shines it onto the film. Between the lens and the film is a shutter. When you take a photograph, the shutter opens to let light hit the film. Most cameras also have extra parts, either to help you take better photographs or to enable the camera to take photographs automatically, without you having to adjust the controls.

Disposable cameras come with the film already inside. You take the entire camera to the film processor when the film is used up.

Compact camera

A compact camera is a small camera that fits in your pocket. To take a photograph, aim at the scene and press the shutter release button. Simple compacts also are called point-and-shoot cameras.

Shutter release button

Viewfinder

Flash unit, to light up dark scenes

Lens protected by plastic flap when camera is not in use

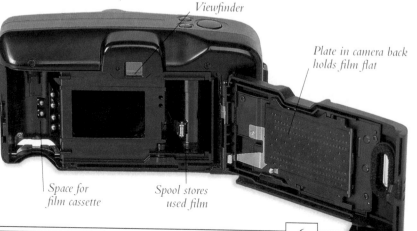

Viewfinder

Plate in camera back holds film flat

Space for film cassette

Spool stores used film

Inside the camera

Open the back of the camera to load and unload the film. There is a space for the film cassette and a spool where the used film is stored. The film is advanced, or wound, either by an electric motor or by hand.

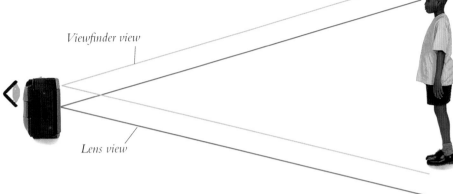

Viewfinder view

Lens view

You look through a viewfinder to see what will be in your photo. Guidelines (indicated here in red) that are found in many viewfinders show what area will be included. Here, the boy's hat will be cropped off.

Close-up care

The view that you see in the viewfinder of a compact camera is not quite the same as the view that the lens sees because the viewfinder is up higher on the camera than the lens and, sometimes, is off to the side. Remember to leave some space around close-up objects in the viewfinder.

Instant photos

With most cameras, you have to send the film away to be developed and made into photographs, or prints. A Polaroid camera *(right)* uses special film and produces prints almost instantly.

Single-lens reflex camera

This type of camera *(left)* is called a single-lens reflex (SLR) camera. When you look into the viewfinder, you actually look through the lens itself, which means you see exactly what the lens sees. You can take a lens off an SLR camera and replace it with another lens.

SLR camera

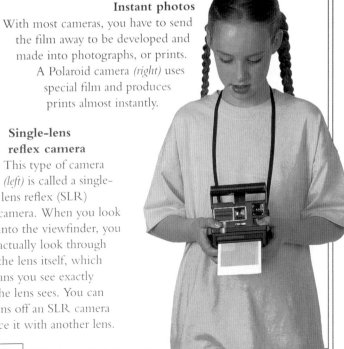

HOW A LENS WORKS

MAKING your own simple viewer will show you just how a camera lens collects light from a scene and makes a small copy of it on the film. The copy is called an image. Just like a real camera, the viewer has a lightproof box. At the front of the box is a pinhole, which works like a tiny lens. The screen at the back of the box is where the film would be in a real camera. This kind of viewer sometimes is called a camera obscura. In the past, artists used the camera obscura to make images of scenes that they could copy in their drawings and paintings.

MATERIALS

You will need: ruler, small cardboard box, scissors, cardboard, sharp pencil, tape, tracing paper.

Light rays
Light travels in straight rays. You can see this when you shine a flashlight. When you look at a scene, your eyes collect rays from every part of it, just like a camera does.

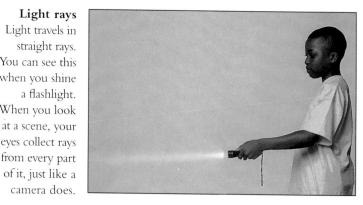

Make your own viewer

1 Draw a 1-inch (2.5-centimeter) square on one end of the cardboard box and cut it out.

2 Cut out a much larger square in the other end of the box.

3 Cut a 2-inch (5-cm) square of cardboard. Pierce a tiny hole in the center with a sharp pencil.

Making an image with light

When you use your viewer, the pinhole lets in just a few light rays from each part of the scene. The rays keep going in straight lines and hit the tracing paper screen, making an image of the scene.

If you look at a person through your viewer, light rays from the person's head hit the bottom of the viewer's screen. Rays from the person's feet hit the top of the screen. The screen image is upside down. Left and right are reversed, too.

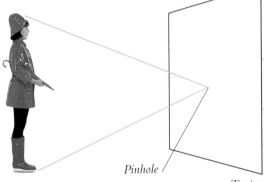

Pinhole

Tracing paper screen

4 Put the cardboard with the tiny hole over the box's smaller opening and tape it in place.

5 Cut a square of tracing paper slightly bigger than the box's larger opening and tape it in place.

6 Now look out a window through the tracing paper screen. Try tracing what you see onto the paper.

REFRACTION AND REFLECTION

A LIGHT ray keeps going in a straight line until it hits something. Then, it usually changes direction by bending or bouncing. When light rays bend, it is called refraction. For example, objects often look distorted when seen through certain types of glass, or through water, because the rays have been bent by the glass or the water. Reflection is the word used to describe light rays that bounce off objects with shiny surfaces, such as mirrors. How does all this apply to cameras? Camera lenses are made of specially shaped pieces of glass. They refract light rays in an organized way, turning them into a clear image on the film and producing the picture in your viewfinder. Some cameras also have carefully angled mirrors off of which rays bounce in a specific direction.

Light rays from the part of the straw that is under water bend as they pass through the surface, making the straw look bent.

Magnifying lens
A magnifying glass lens has a convex shape, which means that its faces curve outward. This shape makes the light rays passing through the lens converge.

Converging light rays
The lens of a magnifying glass makes light rays from objects converge, or bend inward, toward each other. So, when the light rays enter the eye, they seem to have come from a bigger object.

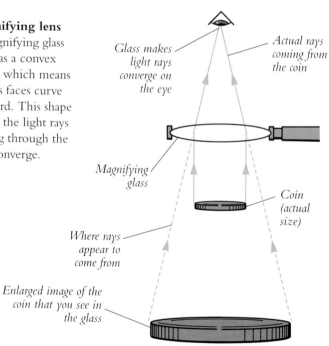

Glass makes light rays converge on the eye

Actual rays coming from the coin

Magnifying glass

Coin (actual size)

Where rays appear to come from

Enlarged image of the coin that you see in the glass

Camera lenses

A magnifying glass is a single converging lens, but some camera lenses consist of several lenses. Each lens is called an element, and the light passes through all of them. Multiple-element lenses, like the ones seen here *(right)*, help prevent your images from having colored edges, which is a particularly common problem with single-element lenses.

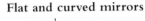

Flat and curved mirrors

Some cameras have one or more mirrors instead of a lens. All the rays that hit a mirror are reflected. A flat mirror *(left)* reflects all rays in the same way, so your image looks unchanged (although left and right seem reversed).

A convex mirror reflects and bends light *(right)*. It works like a mirror and a lens together to distort the image.

Film

Light rays

Lens

How a camera makes images

All camera lenses are converging lenses. They bend light rays from the scene inward toward each other. The light rays from any given part of your subject are bent so that they meet again on the other side of the lens. In a camera, they meet on the film.

EXPERIMENT WITH LIGHT

THE best way to see refraction and reflection at work is to create some light beams and send them through lenses and bounce them off mirrors. You can make narrow light beams by shining a flashlight through slots in pieces of cardboard. Try these experiments, and come up with some ideas of your own. Carry out the experiments in a room with the lights off and the shades down or curtains drawn. Pale-colored cardboard will work most effectively.

Having fun with beams

1 Cut slots about $\frac{1}{8}$ inch (3 millimeters) wide and 2 inches (5 cm) long in two pieces of cardboard. Shine a flashlight through both slots to make a beam of light. *(These pictures are in the light to show you what is happening, but you will get the best effects in the dark.)*

2 Now put a glass of water in the path of the beam. Move the glass from side to side to see how the beam is refracted, more or less.

3 Replace the second piece of cardboard with one that has three slots cut in it. Put a magnifying glass in the path of the three beams to make them converge.

Clear images

See how an SLR gives crisp images. Hold up a glass of water so that you can see the underneath surface of the water clearly. Now poke your finger into the water from above. You should see a clear, single reflection of your finger in the surface because the surface acts like a mirror.

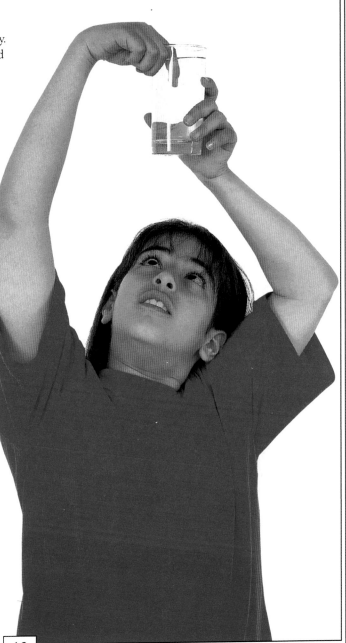

MIRRORS AND PRISMS

Stopping reflections

If you look very carefully at a reflection in a normal mirror, you can see a ghostly second image. The water mirror (described *above*) does not make a ghost image. To prevent ghost images, the SLR has a glass block called a pentaprism, which treats reflections in the same way as the water.

The same view

The pentaprism in an SLR camera also ensures that the image you see in the viewfinder is the same as the image you see on your final photo.

4 Now put a mirror in the path of the different beams. Can you see how the pattern of rays stays the same?

GETTING INTO FOCUS

Before taking a photograph, you need to make sure that your subject is in focus. When it is, all the rays of light that leave a point on the subject are bent by the lens so they hit the same place on the film to make a clear, sharp image of the subject. Parts of the scene in front of or behind the subject might not be in sharp focus. You can choose the part of the scene that you want to be in focus. This is known as depth of field. On some cameras, you have to do the focusing yourself, but autofocus cameras do it automatically.

In the photograph (above), the subject is in sharp focus. You can see all the fine detail. When the same shot is out of focus (right), it makes the subject look blurred.

Getting closer
Use a magnifying glass and a lamp to make an image of an object on a sheet of paper. Move the magnifying glass toward and away from the paper to bring different parts of the scene into focus.

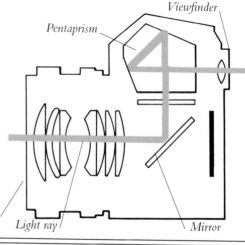

Focal plane

The focal plane
When the image of a subject is in focus, the light rays meet on a flat area called the focal plane. The camera's film is held flat in the focal plane. You can see the focal plane if you open the back of your camera.

Focusing SLRs
With an SLR camera, you see exactly what the image looks like through the viewfinder. On a manual-focus SLR, you turn a ring on the lens to get your subject in focus.

Viewfinder

Pentaprism

Lens

Light ray

Mirror

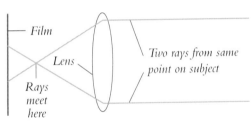

Film

Lens

Two rays from same point on subject

Rays meet here

The lens is too far from the film. Rays meet in front of the film, so the subject is out of focus.

In and out of focus

A camera focuses by moving the lens backward and forward, so it is closer to or farther away from the film. Doing this brings parts of the scene that are at different distances from the camera into focus.

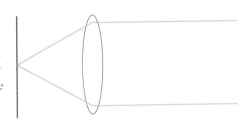

To focus, the lens is moved backward, toward the film. The rays meet on the film.

Autofocus

With this autofocus system *(right)*, the camera emits a wide beam of invisible infrared light. By figuring out how long it takes this light to bounce back, it knows how far away the subject is. Then, a small electric motor moves the lens toward or away from the film.

Yellow lines = beam traveling out to subject from camera
Red lines = beam bouncing back to camera from subject

Sends out beam

Top view of camera

Detector

Autofocus errors

Most autofocus cameras focus on objects that are in the center of the scene in the viewfinder. If your subject is off to one side, the camera focuses on the background, and your subject will be blurred *(left)*. If you have a focus lock, you can beat the autofocus by aiming at the subject first, then using your focus lock before recomposing the shot and shooting *(right)*.

USING FILM

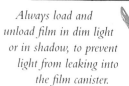

THE camera's job is to create a focused image of a scene, but this image is of no use without a way to record it. Recording the image is the film's job. Film contains chemicals that are affected by light. The more light that hits them, the more they are changed. So, when an image hits the film, the chemicals record the patterns of light, dark, and color. Film must be developed with chemicals before the image shows up. Until it is developed, it must be kept in the dark or the film will react to light and be ruined.

Always load and unload film in dim light or in shadow, to prevent light from leaking into the film canister.

Types of film

There are several different types of film. The most common type is film for color prints. This is called color negative film. Other common types are slide (color reversal) film and black-and-white negative film.

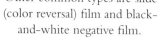

Exposing film

Black-and-white film contains millions of microscopic light-sensitive crystals. These crystals contain silver. When a photograph is taken, some of the crystals that are exposed to light begin to break down, leaving metal silver. Where more light falls, more crystals begin to change.

Film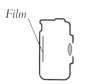

Film is exposed by the camera when a photo is taken of a bird on a light background (left).

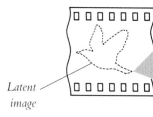 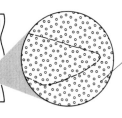

Latent image

Crystals in this area exposed to light

Crystals in the light area of the image change (above). Crystals in the dark area do not. The image has been recorded chemically. Nothing shows up on the film, and the image is called the latent image.

Processing film

Amateur photographers can develop black-and-white film at home. In a dark place, the film is wound onto a plastic spiral, which is placed in a small developing tank. A lid is put on the tank, and a chemical called developer is poured in, left for a few minutes, and poured out. Stop bath is used to stop the developing. Then, a chemical fixer is poured in. Finally, the film is washed.

Film drying

After washing, films are carefully dried. They usually are hung up to dry in a dust-free area, sometimes in a special drying cabinet. When the films are dry, the photographer can examine them and choose the ones to print.

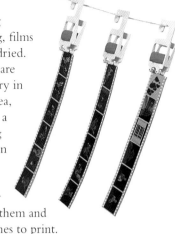

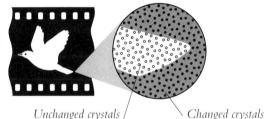

Black background with white bird

Unchanged crystals / *Changed crystals*

During developing (above), *all the crystals that had begun to break down change completely to silver. They look black. The unchanged crystals stay as they are.*

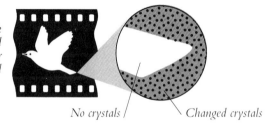

Black background with clear bird

No crystals / *Changed crystals*

Fixing (above) *gets rid of all the unchanged crystals, leaving clear film. The result is a negative, where dark areas on the original subject are light, and light areas are dark.*

Color negative film does not present true colors. The true colors are revealed when prints are made.

When slide film is developed, the actual colors of the scene are reproduced.

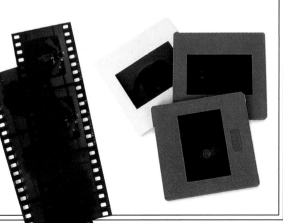

THE RIGHT FILM

The three basic types of film are color negative film, color slide film, and black-and-white negative film. Film comes in different sizes, called formats, and most cameras require 35-mm (millimeter) roll film. Film also comes in different lengths. The lengths are measured by the number of exposures, or photographs, that will fit on the film. The usual lengths are 24 and 36 exposures. Film comes in different speeds, too. Fast films react to light more quickly than slow films. Film speed is called the ISO rating. The most common speeds are ISO 100 and ISO 200, which are medium-speed films.

Details of each film (format, length, and speed) are written on the film carton and the film cassette.

Automatic coding
On one side of a film cassette is a pattern of black and silver squares called a DX code. This code indicates the film's ISO rating and length. Modern cameras have special sensors that can read the code. On older cameras, you have to set the ISO rating on a dial.

Which film speed?
The difference between films of different speeds is the size of their crystals, or grains. Fast films (ISO 400 and above) are perfect for shots in dim light and for action shots. They have larger grains than slow films because larger grains can react to much less light than small ones. These large grains often show up in the final picture *(above, right)*. Slow films (ISO 50 and below) are perfect for fine, crisp detail *(above, left)*.

120 film

35-mm film

APS film

Disk camera film

110 film

126 film

Film and photo formats

Format is the size of the film and the size and shape of each image recorded on the film. Large-format films give much more detail. Smaller formats are more convenient. Some cameras can take photographs of different formats on the same film.

Indoor film

Most color films are designed for use in daylight. If you use them indoors, with light from a flash, the photos come out yellowish. You can buy special indoor film, called tungsten film, which produces better colors.

Winding on

Roll films have a row of small holes along each side. These holes fit over sprockets inside the camera, which turn to advance the film after a photo has been taken, bringing a fresh piece of unexposed film into place behind the lens.

Film with holes along edge

Sprockets

Used film stored on spool

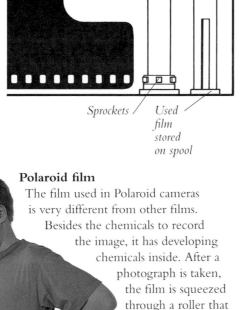

Polaroid film

The film used in Polaroid cameras is very different from other films. Besides the chemicals to record the image, it has developing chemicals inside. After a photograph is taken, the film is squeezed through a roller that releases the developer, turning the film into a finished photograph.

FACT BOX

• Infrared film is special film with chemicals that react to the invisible heat from a scene, rather than to the scene's visible light.

• The largest negative ever used measured 21 feet (6.4 meters) by 1 foot (30.5 cm). This massive negative was made for a huge panoramic picture of 3,500 people in the United States in 1992.

• 35-mm format film originally was designed for movie cameras.

RECORDING AN IMAGE

Y OU do not need a camera to see how film works. In fact, you do not need film either! You can use black-and-white photographic paper instead. Photographic paper is the paper that prints are made on. It works in the same way as film. Here, you can see how to make a picture called a photogram. It is made by covering some parts of a sheet of photographic paper with objects and then shining light on the sheet. When the paper is developed, the areas that were hit by the light turn black.

You will need: lamp, photographic paper, various objects (such as keys, washers, and scissors), rubber gloves, protective goggles, plastic tongs, plastic pans or trays, chemicals (see below).

Photographic chemicals
You will need three photographic chemicals – developer (for paper, not film), stop bath (or diluted vinegar), and fixer. You can buy them from a photographic supplier. With an adult's help, follow the instructions on the bottles to dilute the chemicals. Store them in a cool place in sealed and clearly labeled, opaque, plastic bottles.

Make your own photogram

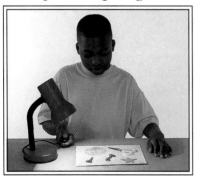

1 In a dark room, place objects on the smooth side of a sheet of photographic paper. Turn on the lamp – for a few seconds only!

2 Wearing gloves and goggles, use tongs to slide the paper into a pan of developer. Push the paper completely under the liquid.

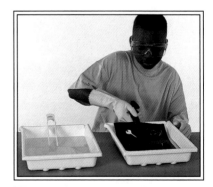

3 After a minute or two, move the paper into the stop bath for fifteen seconds. Then move it into the fixer for two or three minutes.

Photographic paper

For black-and-white prints, you need a paper called monochrome paper. Buy the smallest size you can and choose Grade 2, if possible, with a gloss finish. The paper comes in a lightproof envelope. Open the envelope only in complete darkness.

This symbol on photographic chemical bottles means that the chemicals can be dangerous if not used with care. Always wear gloves and goggles.

The finished photogram should show the objects in white on a black background. Try experimenting with other ideas. How about cutting out letters and making your name?

4 Now you can turn on the light. Lift the paper out of the fixer and wash it with cool running water for a few minutes. Lay the paper flat to dry.

THE CAMERA SHUTTER

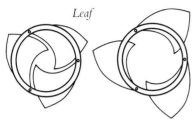
Leaf

A leaf shutter has thin metal plates, called leaves, that overlap each other to close the shutter (left) and swivel back to open it (right).

ALL cameras have a shutter between the lens at the front and the film at the back. The shutter is like a door. It is closed most of the time, so that no light gets to the film. When you take a photo, the shutter opens, then closes again, to let light from your subject reach the film. The length of time the shutter is open is called the shutter speed. Compact cameras have a leaf shutter close to the lens. SLR cameras, which have interchangeable lenses, have a focal-plane shutter, just in front of the film.

First curtain

Focal-plane shutter
A focal-plane shutter has two curtains. The first curtain opens to let light hit the film. The second curtain follows closely behind to cover up the film again. The smaller the gap between the curtains, the faster the shutter speed.

Second curtain

Shutter speeds
Most photographs are taken with a shutter speed between 1/60 and 1/250 of a second. On some SLR cameras, you have to set the shutter speed by turning a dial. Each setting gives a shutter speed about twice as fast as the one before.

Camera shake
When the shutter is open, even tiny camera movements may cause a blurred image. These movements are called camera shake.

A tripod forms a steady base for a camera. It is very useful if you are taking photographs with slow shutter speeds because there is no chance of camera shake. Using a tripod also will help you compose your pictures well because you do not have to worry about holding the camera.

There are several ways to keep your camera steady as you take a photograph, even if you do not have a tripod. For example, stand with your legs slightly apart or crouch down with one knee on the ground. Squeeze the shutter release button slowly. For extra steadiness, lean against a wall, or try resting your camera on a wall.

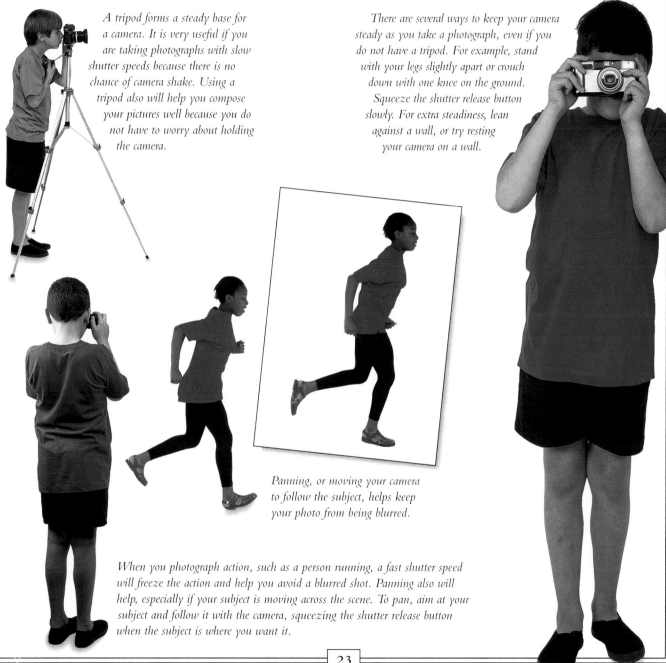

Panning, or moving your camera to follow the subject, helps keep your photo from being blurred.

When you photograph action, such as a person running, a fast shutter speed will freeze the action and help you avoid a blurred shot. Panning also will help, especially if your subject is moving across the scene. To pan, aim at your subject and follow it with the camera, squeezing the shutter release button when the subject is where you want it.

THE APERTURE

The aperture ring on an SLR lens. Aperture size is measured in f-numbers (such as f/8).

MOST cameras have an aperture as well as a shutter. The aperture is, basically, a hole behind the camera lens that can be made larger or smaller. When the aperture is small, some of the light rays that pass through the lens are cut off and do not reach the film. None of the image is cut off on the film, but, because a reduced amount of light hits the film, the image is darker. A longer shutter speed is needed to make up for this loss of light. Changing the size of the aperture also affects how much of a scene is in focus.

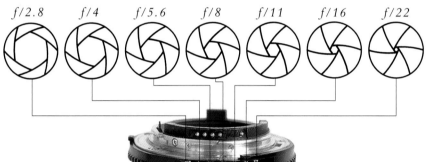

f/2.8   f/4   f/5.6   f/8   f/11   f/16   f/22

Aperture sizes

The mechanism that changes aperture size has interlocking metal leaves that fold in to make the aperture smaller. The f-number is a fraction – f/4 means a quarter of the focal length of the lens. So, an aperture of f/8 is half the width of an aperture of f/4 and lets in one quarter the amount of light.

Changing depth of field

Depth of field is the distance between the nearest part of the scene that is in focus and the farthest part of the scene that is in focus. As f-numbers get bigger, the aperture gets smaller and the depth of field increases. Taking pictures on a sunny day will let you use a small aperture, making it easier to get a large depth of field.

f/2.8

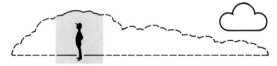

f/8

f/16

In this photograph, the subject is in focus, and the background is totally out of focus. It has a shallow depth of field because only objects a certain distance from the camera are in focus. Using shallow depth of field is ideal if you want to make parts of the scene that might confuse your picture disappear into a blur.

This photograph was taken with a much smaller aperture than the photograph on the left, making the depth of field far deeper. Almost everything in the scene is in focus. Greater depth of field is useful for photographs of scenery, especially if you have people in the foreground.

Try focusing your camera at a certain object and then changing the aperture. You will see how different areas of the picture come into focus. The depth of field falls approximately 1/3 in front of the object and 2/3 behind. The depths of field (below) will change depending on the focal length of the lens.

FACT BOX

• A lens always has its maximum aperture written on it. For example, a lens described as 300 f/4 has a focal length of 300 mm (12 inches) and a maximum aperture of f/4.

• Large maximum apertures tend to be very expensive because the lenses have to be much bigger! An f/1.4 lens, for example, can cost several times as much as an f/4 lens.

• A pinhole camera that is approximately the size of a shoe box has an aperture of about f/500.

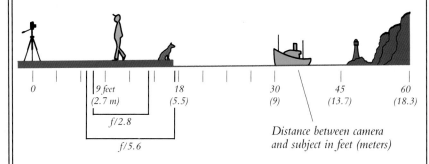

| 0 | 9 feet (2.7 m) | 18 (5.5) | 30 (9) | 45 (13.7) | 60 (18.3) |

f/2.8

f/5.6

Distance between camera and subject in feet (meters)

| *Depths of field for different aperture sizes with the lens focused at 9 feet (2.7 m):* | *Aperture at:* f/2.8 f/5.6 | *Depth of field:* = 4.5 feet (1.4 m) = 10.5 feet (3.2 m) |

THE RIGHT EXPOSURE

Here, too little light has reached the film, and the chemicals in the film have not reacted enough, causing underexposure. The photo looks too dark.

EXPOSURE is the word for the amount of light that gets to the film in your camera when you take a photograph. Exposure depends on the shutter speed (slower shutter speeds allow more light through) and the aperture (larger apertures also allow more light through). You might see exposure stated as a combination of shutter speed and aperture, for example, 1/60 sec at f/16. All but the simplest cameras measure the amount of light coming from the scene and figure out what exposure is needed for the speed of the film in the camera. They do this with an electronic light sensor called a metering system.

Here, too much light has reached the film, and the chemicals in the film have reacted too much, causing overexposure. The photo looks washed out.

When this photograph was taken, exactly the right amount of light reached the film, giving the correct exposure. The photo is well-balanced – neither too light nor too dark.

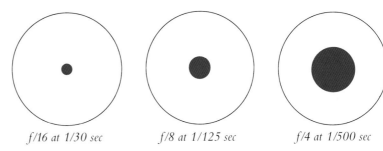

| f/16 at 1/30 sec | f/8 at 1/125 sec | f/4 at 1/500 sec |

Shutter speed and aperture

Try using different combinations of shutter speed and aperture, each of which lets in the same amount of light *(above)*. For example, 1/125 seconds at f/8 is the same as 1/500 seconds at f/4 – the faster shutter speed is paired with a larger aperture. The combination you use depends on the type of photo you want. You might need a fast shutter speed for an action shot or a small aperture for good depth of field in a landscape shot.

In this picture, the background is brighter than the main subject – the girl. The camera measured only the light that is coming from the brighter area. As a result, the background is correctly exposed, but the girl is underexposed and looks too dark.

In this picture, the background is still, by far, the brightest part of the picture, but the problem was solved by metering the main subject – the girl – to get the correct exposure. Bright lighting coming from the background is called back lighting.

LETTING IN THE LIGHT

USE a magnifying glass to investigate how changing a camera's aperture affects both the brightness of an image and the depth of field. To see an aperture at work, look at your own eyes. Like an aperture, your pupils automatically narrow in bright light, to protect your retinas, and open wide, to let you see in dim light. To see a shutter at work, open the back of your camera (when there is no film inside). Look for a leaf shutter near the lens or for a focal-plane shutter in front of the film area.

MATERIALS

You will need: magnifying glass, cardboard tube, tape, thin cardboard, tracing paper, lamp, scissors.

Use your eyes

Look closely at one of your eyes in a mirror. Close it and, after a few seconds, open it again quickly. You should see your pupil go from wide to narrow as your eye detects the bright light.

Apertures

1 Carefully attach the magnifying glass to one end of the cardboard tube with tape.

2 Tape a piece of thin cardboard around the other end of the tube to make another tube that slides back and forth over the tube inside.

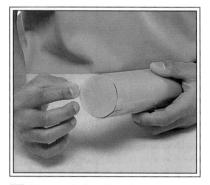

3 Tape a circle of tracing paper across the end of the sliding cardboard tube. The tracing paper is your viewing screen.

See a shutter at work

To see just how a shutter works, open the back of your camera (when there is no film inside) and carefully place a small strip of tracing paper where the film usually goes. Now aim the camera at a subject, preferably one that is brightly lit, and press the shutter release button. You should see a brief flash of the image on your tracing paper.

4 With the viewing screen nearest to you, aim the tubes at a lamp that is turned on. Can you see an image of the bulb on the screen?

5 Adjust the tubes until the image of the bulb is clear. Then, adjust them again so that the image is slightly out of focus.

6 Cut a hole, about ¼ inch (6 mm) wide, in a piece of cardboard to make a small aperture. Look at the light bulb again with the cardboard in front of the lens. The smaller aperture will bring the light bulb into focus.

PRINTING

W HEN film is developed, the images on the film usually are too small to look at. You can view slide films with a projector, which makes a large copy of the image on a screen. Before you can look at photographs taken with negative film, however, you have to make prints. The paper used for prints is light-sensitive, just like film. To make a print, the negative image is projected onto the paper. When the paper is developed, you get a negative of the negative (a positive), so that the scene appears as you saw it originally.

If you are using black-and-white film, remember that bright areas of the image change the chemicals in the film more than dark areas.

Negatives
When black-and-white film is processed, light areas of the scene appear dark, and dark areas appear light. This is a negative.

Enlarging
This picture *(below)* shows the first stage in making a print. An enlarger projects the negative onto paper placed below it. Enlarging must be done in the dark because light will spoil the paper. Lighter areas of the negative let more light get to the paper than darker areas.

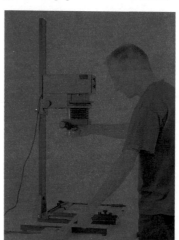

Developing and fixing
The paper is processed in the dark, with chemicals *(above)*. Areas where light has hit the paper come out dark, as in the original scene. *(Note: these pictures look red because they have been taken in a photographer's dark room under safe light conditions.)*

The final print
After processing, the print must be dried to keep it from being damaged.

Color photos

When you take a photo with color negative film, the film records the patterns of color in a scene. When the film is developed, the colors on the film do not look true, but the prints come out correctly. All color films have at least three layers (a few have four layers), one on top of the other, that can react to all of the different colors in the light spectrum.

Printing in color

Color prints are produced in the same way as black-and-white prints. The negative *(above)* is projected onto color photographic paper. When the paper is developed, the colors are reversed, once again, so that they come out looking natural.

FACT BOX

• The negative/positive method of photography was invented in 1839 by an Englishman named William Fox Talbot.

• High-contrast printing paper makes blacks look blacker and whites look whiter. Low-contrast paper creates less of a difference between black and white.

• Professionals can make certain areas of a print look darker or lighter by using special techniques with the enlarger. Burning lets in more light to make areas darker; dodging uses less light to make areas lighter.

Processing and printing

Most people have their films processed and printed *(right)* by a photographic laboratory. Some stores even have their own automatic processing and printing machines that can produce prints on the spot in a very short time.

YOUR OWN CAMERA

Y OU can make your very own simple camera with just a few basic pieces of equipment. This project combines all the main principles of photography. For simplicity, this camera uses photographic paper instead of film and a pinhole instead of a lens. When the film (paper) is processed, you will have a negative. Then, turn to pages 34 and 35 to find out how you can make a print from the negative. Find out about the equipment you need by referring to pages 20 and 21.

Make a pin-hole camera

turn to pages 34 and 35 ... referring to pages 20 and 21.

M A T E R I A L S

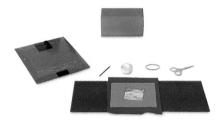

You will need: pinhole box viewer, aluminum foil, pencil, black paper, thin cardboard, scissors, tape, lightproof cloth or plastic, photographic paper, rubber band.

1 Make a pinhole viewer as shown on pages 8 and 9, but do not add the tracing-paper screen. Replace the cardboard square with foil. Use a pencil to poke a hole, ⅛ inch (3 mm) across, in the center of the foil.

2 Cover as much of the inside of the box as you can with black paper, or color the inside of the box with a black felt-tip marker.

3 Cut a square of thin cardboard large enough to cover the foil. Tape only one edge to the box to make a flap that will act as a shutter.

4 Cut another square of cardboard to fit across the other end of the box. Tape it to one edge so that it closes over the hole like a door.

5 Cut a piece of lightproof cloth or plastic large enough to fold over the end of the box.

6 In a completely dark room, put a piece of photographic paper under the flap at the end of the box. *(Note: these pictures are red because they were taken in a dark room under safe light conditions.)*

7 Close the flap, wrap the cloth over it, and put a rubber band around the cloth to keep it in place.

8 Now turn the light on. Point the camera at a well-lit object and open the shutter. Leave the camera still for about five minutes, then close the shutter.

Following these steps will give you a negative on paper instead of on film. To develop the negative into a positive, follow the instructions given on pages 34 and 35.

PRINTING AND PROJECTING

I F you have just taken a photograph with your own pinhole camera, this project will help you turn it into a print. You also can make a simple projector. A projector lets you look at slide film – a type of film on which the colors of the image on the processed film are the same as the colors in the original scene. You can think of projecting a photographic image as the reverse of taking a picture. First, light is shined right through the film. Then the light goes through the lens of the projector and is focused on a screen, forming a large copy of your image.

MATERIALS

You will need: photographic paper, negative from a pinhole camera, flashlight or lamp, safety goggles, rubber gloves, plastic pans, chemicals, plastic tongs or tweezers.

A slide viewer is a special magnifying glass used for looking at slides. It is a convenient alternative to a projector.

Quick and easy prints

1 In a totally dark room, lay a fresh sheet of photographic paper on a flat surface, shiny side up. Lay the negative from your pinhole camera face-down on top of the paper.

2 Shine a flashlight or a lamp over the top of the two papers for a few seconds. Turn the light off and remove your paper negative. Put on the goggles and gloves.

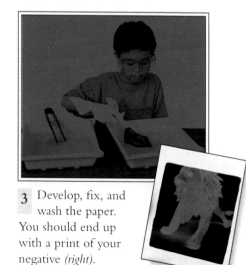

3 Develop, fix, and wash the paper. You should end up with a print of your negative *(right)*.

Do-it-yourself projector

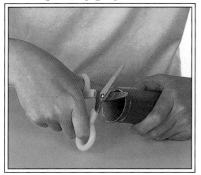

1 Cut two slits in the sides of the cardboard tube at one end so that a strip of negatives will slide through. Use only old negatives that you do not want prints from anymore.

2 Tape thin cardboard around the other end of the tube to make another tube that slides backward and forward over the first one.

3 Tape the magnifying glass to the end of the outside tube. Tape a circle of tracing paper over the slotted end of the inside tube.

4 Hold the projector about 6 feet (2 m) from a light-colored wall. Shine a flashlight through the negative and adjust the tubes until an image of the negative appears on the wall. You can try this with slide film, also, but use only old, unwanted slides.

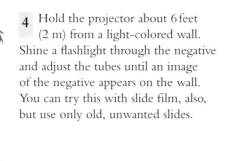

MATERIALS

You will need: a cardboard tube, scissors, developed color negative film, thin cardboard, tape, magnifying glass, tracing paper, flashlight.

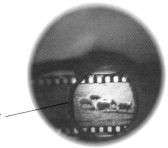

The projected image

WIDE AND NARROW

What the lens sees
Put your hands on either side of your face. Your view is similar to what a 50-mm lens can see.

Aᴸᴸ camera lenses have their own focal length, which is written somewhere on the lens. The focal length is the distance between the center of the lens and the focal plane where it creates an image of a distant object. Lenses of different focal lengths produce images on the film that contain more or less of a scene. If you look in the viewfinder of a 35-mm camera with a 50-mm lens, you see about the same amount of the scene as you do with your eyes. Lenses with shorter focal lengths take in more of the scene, and longer lenses take in less.

Long-lens wobble
With telephoto lenses, which have very long focal lengths (300 mm or more), the tiniest bit of camera shake blurs the image. Professionals always use a tripod or monopod with these lenses to keep the camera steady. Some long lenses even have gyroscopes built in to help stabilize them.

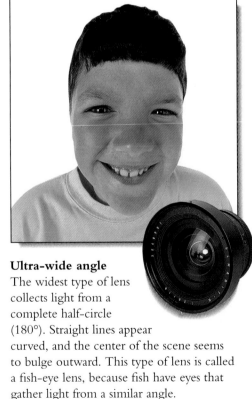

Ultra-wide angle
The widest type of lens collects light from a complete half-circle (180°). Straight lines appear curved, and the center of the scene seems to bulge outward. This type of lens is called a fish-eye lens, because fish have eyes that gather light from a similar angle.

Compacts

Some compact cameras have lenses that give wide and narrow views. The simplest compacts have a 35-mm lens, which gives a slightly wider view *(left)* than you see with your own eyes.

Compact camera with variable lens

A wide-angle lens view

Wide-angle lenses

Any camera lens that gives a wider view than we usually see with our eyes is called a wide-angle lens. Extremely wide-angle lenses (28-mm and less) allow you to get a huge amount of a scene into your photograph. A really large wide-angle lens is perfect to use for panoramic photographs of scenery, such as landscapes.

A telephoto lens view

Telephoto lens

Any lens that gives you a magnified view of a scene is called a telephoto lens. A telephoto lens is a bit like a telescope because it hones in on just one part of the scene. Telephoto lenses often are used to photograph portraits and distant wildlife and to come in close on the small details in a scene.

GETTING CLOSER

To avoid carrying several different lenses with different focal lengths, many photographers have lenses, called zoom lenses, that can change their focal lengths. A zoom lens allows you to change how much of the scene will be in a shot with the push of a button. The built-in lens on many compact cameras and the lens that comes with most SLRs are zoom lenses. A common zoom is 35-70, which means the lens can have focal lengths between 35 mm and 70 mm. It goes from wide angle to short telephoto (which brings objects closer). Macro, or close-up, lenses can focus on things very close to the lens. They are ideal for close-up shots of flowers and insects.

A compact camera with a built-in zoom lens. Pressing a button on the camera makes the zoom longer or shorter.

SLR zooms

With an SLR and two interchangeable zoom lenses, such as 28-70 and 75-300, you can have a huge range of focal lengths. The focal length is changed by turning or sliding a wide ring on the lens. Because zoom lenses are complicated, they can make straight lines in a scene look slightly bent.

A photograph taken at the 28-mm setting on a 28-200 zoom lens

Super-zooms

A super-zoom lens has a very large range of focal lengths. For example, a 28-200 zoom goes from very wide angle to long telephoto.

Zooming in for detail with a 200-mm setting

Close-up equipment

Special high-powered microscope cameras are used for some extreme close-ups, especially for nature and scientific subjects *(left and right)*.

Extension tubes

An extension tube *(left)* fits between the camera body and the lens. It moves the lens farther from the film so that the lens can bend light rays into focus from objects that usually would be too close. A set of extension tubes has three tubes of different lengths for different magnifications.

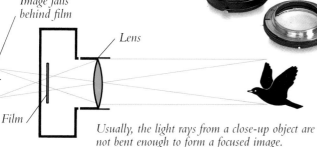

Image falls behind film

Lens

Film

Usually, the light rays from a close-up object are not bent enough to form a focused image.

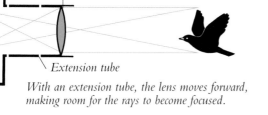

Image focused on film

Lens

Film

Extension tube

With an extension tube, the lens moves forward, making room for the rays to become focused.

FACT BOX

• A telephoto doubler fits between an SLR and its lens. It doubles the focal length of the lens.

• A 500-mm telephoto lens with a maximum aperture of f/8 weighs several pounds (kilograms).

• The longest lenses you can buy have focal lengths of 1000 to 1200 mm.

• A standard 50-mm lens might be made up of 5 glass lenses. Most zoom lenses contain at least 12 lenses.

FOCAL LENGTHS

If you have either an SLR camera or a compact camera with a zoom lens, then you probably will have taken photographs at different focal lengths. The simple experiments shown on these two pages will help explain how different focal lengths make more or less of a scene appear on the film. In the mini-experiment *(left)*, try to find as many convex lenses as you can with which to experiment.

You will find that weaker lenses, which have longer focal lengths, make larger images, which is the opposite of what happens if you use them as a magnifying glass.

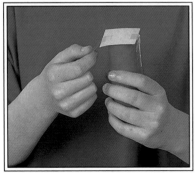

Working with lenses
Standing by a window, use a magnifying glass to form an image of the window on a piece of paper. See what happens when you use different convex lenses.

You will need: cardboard tube, thin cardboard, sharp pencil, tape, tracing paper, scissors.

Zooming in and out

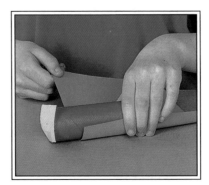

1 Cover one end of a cardboard tube with thin cardboard. Pierce a small hole in the center of the thin cardboard with a sharp pencil.

2 Wrap a piece of thin cardboard around the other end of the tube. Tape the edge down to form a sliding tube.

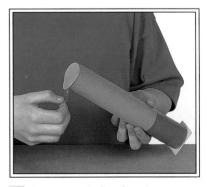

3 Cut out a circle of tracing paper big enough to fit over the end of the outside tube. Tape it firmly in place.

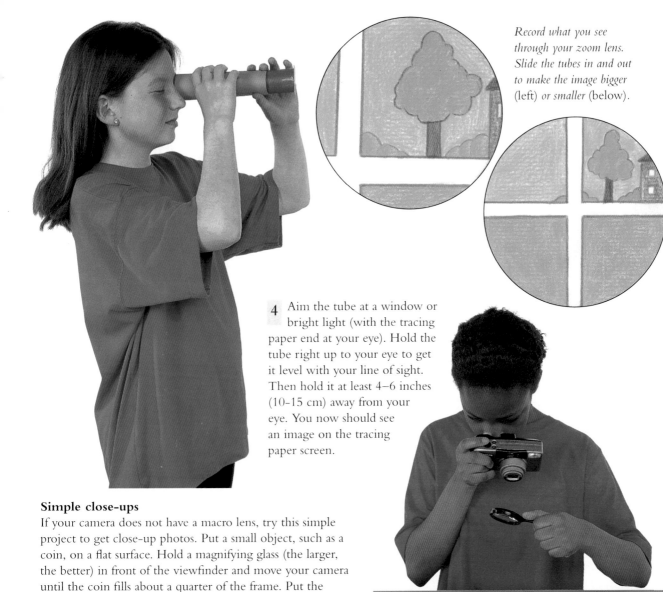

Record what you see through your zoom lens. Slide the tubes in and out to make the image bigger (left) or smaller (below).

4 Aim the tube at a window or bright light (with the tracing paper end at your eye). Hold the tube right up to your eye to get it level with your line of sight. Then hold it at least 4–6 inches (10-15 cm) away from your eye. You now should see an image on the tracing paper screen.

Simple close-ups

If your camera does not have a macro lens, try this simple project to get close-up photos. Put a small object, such as a coin, on a flat surface. Hold a magnifying glass (the larger, the better) in front of the viewfinder and move your camera until the coin fills about a quarter of the frame. Put the magnifying glass in front of the camera lens and take the photograph. Take a few more shots with the camera a bit nearer and, then, a bit farther away from the coin.

LIGHTING AND FLASH

LIGHTING is one of the most important parts of photography. The kind of light you have, how that light hits the subject, and where you take the picture from – all affect the result. Outdoors, most photos are taken with natural light. Artificial light is needed indoors, and outdoors when there is not enough natural light. Although photos can be taken in dim natural light without additional artificial light, exposures usually have to be very long. Lighting also can create dramatic effects. Flash lighting makes a very bright light for a fraction of a second. Most small cameras have a small flash unit built in.

With front lighting, light is coming to the subject from the same direction as the camera. It lights the subject evenly but gives a flat look because there are no strong shadows.

This is an example of side lighting (left) with light coming from both sides. In back lighting, light comes from behind the subject. Back lighting results in a silhouette of the subject.

When the light is at about a 45° angle to the subject and a 45° angle above the camera (left), it will create shadows that give more shape to the subject.

Lights and reflectors

Photographic studios *(left)* have lots of strong lights. They allow the photographer to create many different lighting effects. Some lights cover a wide area, and others make narrow beams. Umbrellas and sheets of reflecting material help direct the light, too.

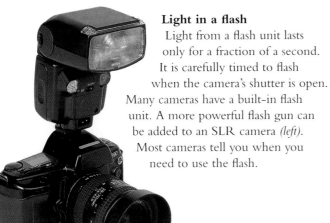

Light in a flash

Light from a flash unit lasts only for a fraction of a second. It is carefully timed to flash when the camera's shutter is open. Many cameras have a built-in flash unit. A more powerful flash gun can be added to an SLR camera *(left)*. Most cameras tell you when you need to use the flash.

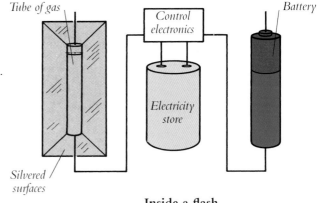

Tube of gas

Control electronics

Battery

Electricity store

Silvered surfaces

Inside a flash

Flash is made by sending a very large electric current through a narrow tube of gas. This makes a lightning-like flash. The flash's battery gradually builds up a store of electricity, which is released very quickly. It is like filling a jug from a dripping tap and then pouring all the water out at once.

These people are sitting at different distances from the flash, so some of them are overexposed, while others are underexposed.

Arrange people so that they all are about the same distance from the camera, which should ensure that everyone gets the proper exposure.

Bouncing and diffusing

Direct flash from the camera to the subject can cause harsh shadows and red-eye (where light bounces back from a person's eyes and makes them look red). Bounce flash means aiming the flash at the ceiling so the light spreads out. A diffuser is a sheet of material, like tissue paper, that softens the light from the flash.

WORKING WITH LIGHT

You can improve many of your photographs by thinking about the lighting before you shoot. For pictures of people, try some of these simple suggestions to light up their faces in new ways. Outside, move your subject around to study how the light falls on it from different directions. Choose the best position before you take your photo. Ask people you are photographing to position themselves so the sunlight lights up their faces. If this is not possible, some cameras have a back-light button that lengthens the exposure time for dark subjects. You also could add some flash, called fill-in flash, to light up the darker areas.

Red-eye is caused by light from a flash unit near the camera lens bouncing off the retina (at the back of the eye) and back into the lens. With SLR cameras, the flash can be moved to one side to avoid red-eye.

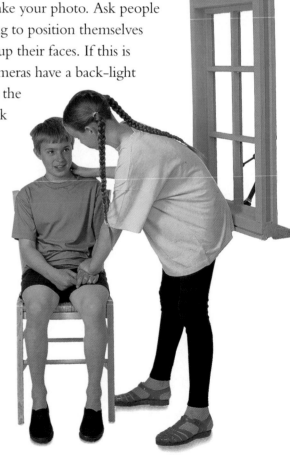

M A T E R I A L S

You will need: a camera, large sheets of white and colored paper or cardboard, aluminum foil, lamp, flashlight, colored tissue paper.

1 Position your subject near a window and ask him or her to turn his or her head in different directions. Move around the room to see the effects of front, side, and back lighting.

2 Hold a sheet of white paper or cardboard near your subject to reflect some light from the window back onto his or her face. The reflected light fills in the shadows caused by the side lighting. If you do this same thing with colored paper, the color will be reflected onto your subject's face.

3 Try the same thing with foil or a piece of shiny cardboard. See how this gives a much brighter reflected light.

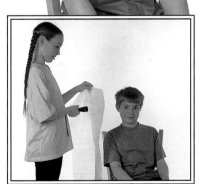

4 For pictures with spooky lighting effects, light your subject from below with an ordinary lamp or a flashlight in a darkened room. If you want to try this kind of effect, you probably will need to ask a friend to help.

5 Take the spooky approach even farther. Experiment with putting your hand in front of the light. With this step, and the previous one, turn off your camera's flash, if you can, and hold the camera very still. If you have a tripod, use it.

6 For less harsh lighting, put a sheet of colored tissue paper in front of the lamp or flashlight. Do not put it *on* the lamp because of the danger of fire. You also can take flash photos with a small piece of tissue paper over the flash unit.

USING FILTERS

APHOTOGRAPHIC filter changes the light as it enters the camera's lens. There are hundreds of different filters, and each one creates its own effect. The most common filter is called a skylight filter. It lets all visible light through the lens but prevents invisible ultraviolet light from getting in. Ultraviolet light can make photographs look unnaturally blue. Filters called graduate filters make some parts of the scene darker. They often are used to darken very bright skies. Colored filters, such as red or yellow, can improve black-and-white photography. There are also many kinds of special-effect filters that you can use to add various effects to your photographs.

Filters are used most frequently with SLR cameras. Some filters are circular and screw onto the end of the camera's lens. Others are designed to slip into a filter holder at the front of the lens.

Bright lights
You will not always want strong reflections and bright light in a picture *(below)*.

Polarizing filter
Putting a special polarizing filter in front of the lens has made the reflections and strong light disappear *(above)*. These filters cut out certain light rays from a scene but let others through. They also can make the sky look more blue.

Creating a sunset

With a sunset filter, you can turn a daytime sky *(above, left)* into a beautiful sunset *(above, right)*. Half the filter is clear and the other half has a slight orange tint. With the tint positioned at the top of your shot, the sky appears orange.

Interesting shapes

A frame filter is a black mask with a shape cut into it. It makes the scene you are shooting come out in the same shape. The other parts of the scene will be black. Frame filters come in simple shapes, such as squares and ovals, and more complex shapes, such as keyholes.

Making your own

Make filters from transparent, colored candy wrappers. Put clean wrappers in front of the viewfinder to see what effect they have. Then attach one to the front of the lens with small pieces of tape and secure it with a rubber band.

USEFUL TIPS

H ERE are a few simple tips that should help you improve your photographic technique and avoid some common mistakes. Good technique is made of technical skill and an eye for an interesting subject. Remember that a complicated SLR camera does not necessarily take the best photographs. Great shots are perfectly possible with a simple point-and-shoot camera. The first thing to decide is the type of film you want to use (color print, color slide, or black-and-white). Always load and unload your film in dim lighting and get it developed quickly after it has been exposed.

Hold a camera steady with both hands. Be careful not to put your fingers over the lens, flash, or autofocus sensor. Squeeze the shutter release button slowly.

Check the background

When you are taking portraits or photographs of groups of people, look in the background as well as at your subject. If necessary, recompose your photo to avoid an unwanted background, such as the wallpaper *(above)*. Many cameras have a special portrait setting that gives a shallow depth of field, which automatically makes the background out of focus.

Fill the frame

Do not be afraid to get close to your subject. If you are taking a portrait, make sure the person's head and shoulders fill the frame *(above, left)*. But be careful not to get too close because the camera may not be able to focus *(above, right)*. If you get too close with an autofocus camera, it will not let you take a picture.

Natural frames
Try adding some interest
to photos by shooting
through archways or
doors to frame the
subject. With many
subjects, interest is added
by including nature
scenes in the shot.

Various positions

Instead of placing a subject directly in the center,
position the subject at various other points across
or up or down the frame – to make the shot more
interesting. With autofocus cameras, you often have
to use your focus lock and point at the subject first,
then recompose the picture before shooting.

A different viewpoint

Photographs taken from a standing
position have the same viewpoint as
your eyes usually do. Changing
the camera's viewpoint can give
more interesting results. Try
kneeling, or even lying down.

Bad-weather photographs

You do not
always need
perfectly sunny
weather before
taking photos. In
fact, overhead
sunshine tends to
result in flat, dull
pictures. Stormy
clouds can be
much more
interesting than
cloudless skies.

SPECIAL PHOTOGRAPHY

Most cameras and lenses are designed for general photography. There are, however, some types of cameras that take photographs in unusual formats or in special conditions. For example, you can use special cameras to take wide panoramic views or to shoot scenes entirely under water. There are also some unusual types of film. Some produce unusual colors or shades in your photographs.

Another type of film records technical information about each of the shots.

Disposable underwater cameras can take photographs while completely under water. The camera's body is recycled after the film is processed.

Underwater SLRs
Divers take photographs under water with special SLR cameras that are waterproof even at great depths. They also can withstand the high pressure of being deep under water.

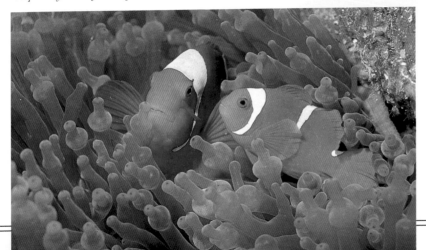

When photographing anything deep under water, extremely bright lights are required.

Panoramic photos

Panoramic cameras take very wide photographs, often of landscapes or large groups of people. Many compact cameras take pictures that are called panoramic but, actually, only appear to be so. They are no wider than a standard frame, just shorter.

Laser photographs

A hologram *(left)* is a three dimensional (3-D) picture that looks 3-D from any angle. The picture changes as you move your head from side to side. Holograms are not taken with a camera but with another type of technological equipment that records how laser light bounces off the subject from different directions.

Advanced systems

Many new compact cameras (and some SLRs) work according to the APS, or the Advanced Photographic System. They use a special type of film that records information about each shot.

AMAZING EFFECTS

Discover how to take stereo photos and how to view them to get an amazing three-dimensional effect. It is easier than you might think, and you can do it with the most basic camera. Simply take two photos of the same scene from different places. The effect works because, like many animals, humans have binocular vision, which means that the two views from our different eyes overlap. In the overlapping area, our eyes see slightly different views, which make things appear in three dimensions. After you have tried this experiment, you can find out how to build a grand panoramic picture of a scene.

Place your stereo pairs of photographs side by side to view them.

Left eye sees this view

Top of head

Right eye sees this view

The diagram at right shows why stereo experiments work – because our two eyes see slightly different views.

The actual 3-D box you are looking at

Make your model come alive

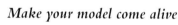

You will need: camera, model.

1 Choose a simple object, such as this model of a dinosaur. Hold the camera very steady and take a picture. Try to include a bit of space around the object.

2 Take a step about 8 inches (20 cm) to your left and take another picture. Try taking more pairs of photographs using different distances between them.

3 Put your pictures down side by side on a flat surface. Place your index finger between them. Look directly down onto the pictures and slowly raise your finger toward your nose, keeping it in focus. The two images should merge into one 3-D image. Try it with these two model dinosaur pictures.

Make a panorama
Choose a general scene with no close-up objects in it. Now, using a camera lens set at 35 or 50 mm, take a series of photographs that overlap slightly. When your prints are developed, lay them out to re-create all of your scene. When you are happy with the arrangement, carefully tape the photos together.

This completed panorama works well because it is a simple, open scene. If it had been filled with small objects, the effect might not have been as good. If you want people in your scene, try to keep them away from areas that will overlap in the finished panorama.

MOVING PICTURES

A movie camera is used to take moving pictures. It takes a whole series of photographs in quick succession (usually about 25 every second) on a very long roll of film. Any moving object appears in a slightly different position in each frame. When the photographs are displayed quickly, one after the other, the movement from the original scene appears to be recreated. The recreation is in the form of transparency film (positive rather than negative film) and is put into a projector to be shown. Today, movie cameras are used mainly for professional filmmaking. Home-movie cameras used to be very popular, but they have been replaced by video cameras.

Moving pictures rely on persistence of vision, which means our eyes remember a picture for a split second. Look around you and quickly close your eyes. Do you remember the scene?

Recording motion

The first movie cameras were made to record and study animal motion, rather than for entertainment. This sequence was taken by British photographer Eadweard Muybridge (1830-1904).

Movie film

Movie film is just like the rolls of film you put in an ordinary camera. In fact, 35-mm film originally was made for movie cameras. The image in each frame of the film is slightly different from the one before.

Inside a movie camera

A movie camera has parts similar to a normal camera – a lens, shutter, and aperture. It also has some extra parts for taking photos in quick succession. The film is wound on, ready for the next frame, while the shutter is closed *(right)*. The shutter speed is always the same and the exposure is controlled just by the aperture.

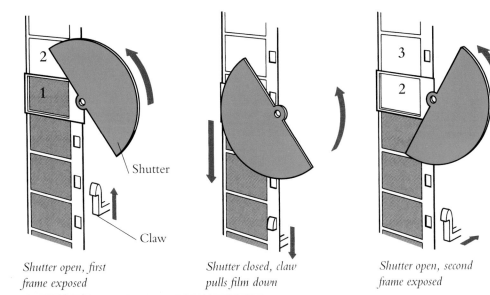

Shutter open, first frame exposed

Shutter closed, claw pulls film down

Shutter open, second frame exposed

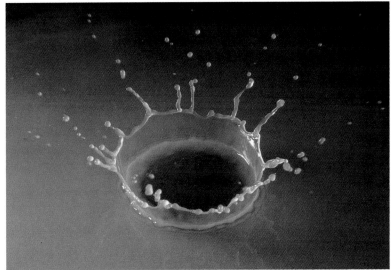

High-speed photos

This picture is a frame from a high-speed film. Some movie cameras can take hundreds, or even thousands, of photographs every second. When they are played back at normal speed, the action is slowed down.

FACT BOX

• The world's fastest camera is the Imacon camera. A sequence of a billion images can be taken in one second!

• If a high-speed camera were used to film a bullet fired from a gun, the bullet would take 1,000 frames to move only 0.04 inch (1 mm).

• Like normal camera film, movie camera film comes in different formats. The most common format is 35-mm.

• In an IMAX movie theater, the screen is as high as seven elephants on top of each other.

• On IMAX film, the frames are four times larger than 35-mm film.

ANIMATION

Animation is making inanimate objects, or objects that cannot move by themselves, appear to move. Frames of the film are photographed, one at a time, with a special movie camera. Between each frame, the objects are moved slightly. When the finished film is viewed, the objects seem to move. Some animated objects are models that are photographed to make animated movies. Others are drawings that are photographed to make cartoons. Cartoon animation often is done by computer, so the photography stage is not needed.

Photo flick-book
The simplest way to make moving pictures is to put all the frames into a book and flick through the pages. In the nineteenth century, flick-books of photographs, called filoscopes, were popular toys. The figures *(above)* are from the pages of an old filoscope.

This picture (right) *shows a scene from one of the very popular* Wallace and Gromit *films, made in Europe by Aardman Animations, Ltd. Model animation is a highly-skilled and time-consuming job. The models are moved only very slightly between each frame.*

Background cels

Cartoon cels

Until the 1980s, animated films were made by photographing drawings. The drawings were done on transparent plastic sheets called cels. Moving characters were drawn on one cel, and the still background on another, to save drawing the background again and again for each frame *(right)*. After the cels were completed, they were photographed with a movie camera. When they were shown in rapid succession, an animated film resulted.

Character cels (notice how each one is different)

Enjoying animation

Today, watching animated films is a very popular pastime. Much of animation is now done with the aid of computers. The computers do all the time-consuming drawing and painting. They also can produce complex, three-dimensional characters or add cartoon elements to films with real actors.

FACT BOX

• A movie camera used for shooting cels is fixed so that it looks down on a flat baseboard. The cels for one frame are placed on the board, and a photo is taken. Then the cels for the next frame are shot, and so on.

• Model animation is done with a rostrum camera, which is held firmly so it does not shift between frames. However, it can be tilted, panned (moved to follow a moving object), and zoomed.

• With model animation, there are approximately 25 frames for every second of finished film.

This little picture appears in the top right-hand corner of every other page. Flick all the pages of the book quickly and watch the pictures. What happens?

EASY ANIMATION

D URING the nineteenth century, there was a craze for optical toys, such as flick-books. Many of the books created an illusion of movement by displaying a sequence of pictures in quick succession. At first, the pictures were hand-drawn. Then, photos taken by early movie cameras were used as well. Here, you can find out how to make a toy called a phenakistoscope and how to use it to turn a series of pictures into animation. This toy is slightly different from the Victorian one *(left)*. The slots on the one you will make are on the outside.

A nineteenth century phenakistoscope. Each image is slightly different. When you spin the circle, you see an action sequence through the slots.

Make your own phenakistoscope

MATERIALS

You will need: cardboard, ruler, scissors, light-colored paper, pencil, tape, model(s), camera, glue, black felt-tip marker.

1 On cardboard, draw a 10-inch (25-cm) circle with eight segments. Draw slots, 2 inches (5 cm) long and $\frac{1}{4}$ inch (6 mm) wide, at the end of each.

2 Cut out the circle and the slots, *as shown*. Make sure that the slots are no wider than $\frac{1}{4}$ inch (6 mm).

3 On paper, draw a series of eight pictures. They should form a movement sequence. Make sure that your drawings are fairly simple and clear and that they are drawn with a clean, strong line.

4 Tape the pictures to the circle, just under the slots. Push a pencil through the center of the cardboard.

5 Stand in front of a mirror. Hold the circle vertically, with the pictures toward the mirror. Spin the circle and look through the slots. You should see an animated loop of action in the mirror.

Photo phenakistoscope

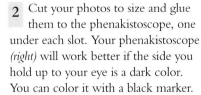

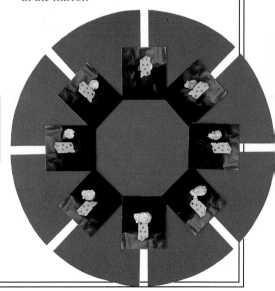

1 Try a model animation. Take eight photographs of a model from the same position. *(Use a tripod, if you can.)* The model should be in the middle third of the photograph frame. Move the model slightly before each shot.

2 Cut your photos to size and glue them to the phenakistoscope, one under each slot. Your phenakistoscope *(right)* will work better if the side you hold up to your eye is a dark color. You can color it with a black marker.

CAMERAS IN SCIENCE

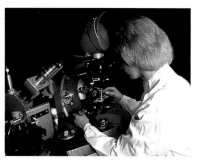

Most of us use our cameras for recording vacations and special occasions or for taking pictures of our family, friends, and pets. Photography also is important in science and technology. For example, it is used to record images that have been made by scientific instruments, so that they can be studied later. It also is used to record experiments that happen too fast for the human eye to see and to analyze experimental results. In many modern scientific instruments, electronic cameras have taken the place of film cameras.

Some special microscopes (above) take very detailed close-up photos. You can do the same thing with a normal microscope by fitting an SLR camera to it. You remove the SLR's lens, and the microscope acts as a close-up lens for the camera.

Their images can be transferred easily to computers for analysis.

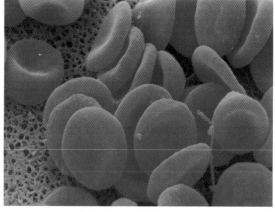

Microscope photographs
A photograph taken with a microscope is called a photomicrograph. This photo-micrograph *(above)* is a close-up of parts of our blood called red blood cells.

Photographing heat
All objects give off heat rays called infrared rays. Hotter objects give off stronger rays. A special type of film called infrared film is sensitive to heat rays rather than light rays. Hot and cold objects show up in different colors or shades.

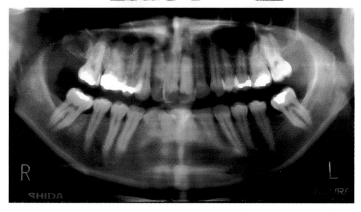

When photos are taken of the night sky with a telescope, using long exposures, the telescope often has to move slowly across the sky to prevent the stars from becoming streaks on the final pictures.

Photographing the stars

Just as a camera can be added to a microscope to take close-up pictures, it also can be added to a telescope. The telescope acts like a very powerful telephoto lens for the camera. (A telephoto lens makes distant objects seem much closer.) Light from the stars is very weak, so long exposures are needed.

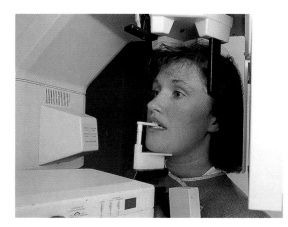

X-ray images

An X-ray picture is simply film that has been processed – a negative. X rays help dentists *(above)* and doctors gain information about the body.

Where X rays reach the film through soft parts of the body, the film turns a dark tone during developing. Bones and teeth (above) appear lighter. The pure white spots are silver fillings.

CAMERAS AND COMPUTERS

Just like ordinary cameras, digital cameras come as compacts and SLRs. They have a lens and shutter, but, in the space where the film normally would be, they have a special light-sensitive microchip that stores the photographs in the camera's memory.

PHOTOGRAPHS often are used in computer applications. For example, a multimedia CD-ROM about nature might contain thousands of photographs of animals and plants. Photographs stored and displayed by computer are called digital images because they consist of a long series of numbers rather than a real photograph on paper. They are either real photographs that have been put into a computer scanner to turn them into digital form, or they have been photographed with a digital, filmless, camera. Digital images can be copied over and over again without any loss in quality, which means they can be sent easily from one computer to another – over the Internet, for example.

FACT BOX

• The highest resolution digital cameras divide a picture into a grid about 7,000 pixels wide and 5,000 pixels deep.

• Many digital pictures use 24-bit color, which means that each pixel can be any one of 16,771,216 different colors.

Video phone

The digital video camera on top of this computer takes pictures that are sent over the telephone line and appear on another computer's screen, letting the people at both computers see each other.

Pixel pictures

A digital image is made up of pixels, or dots. A number represents the color of each tiny dot. High-resolution images divide the picture into a greater number of smaller dots than low-resolution images, but they take up more computer memory.

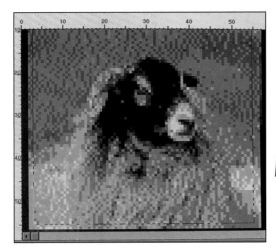

This (above) is a digitized image on a computer screen before it has been manipulated.

Here is the same picture after it has been manipulated by computer. Can you see how it has changed?

Retouching

Once a photo is digitized, it can be altered in any way by computer. For example, colors can be changed or another photo can be added. A polar bear could be put in a desert! It is much easier than accomplishing the same thing with photography.

GLOSSARY

animation – the filming of drawings or objects that cannot move by themselves to make them appear to move.

aperture – the hole in the front of a camera, behind the lens, that lets in light rays to make an image on the film in the back of the camera.

APS – (Advanced Photographic System) a special kind of camera film that has a magnetic layer on which size and setting information about a photo is recorded for use after the film is processed.

binocular vision – the way people (and many animals) see, in which the view from each of our two eyes is slightly different. But because the views overlap, the differences create the three dimensions we actually see.

camera obscura – a camera-like viewer that is a lightproof box that has a small hole in one end to let in light rays that will form the image of an object or subject on a screen at the opposite end of the box, where film would be in a camera.

cels – the see-through plastic sheets that, until recently, cartoon drawings were made on and were photographed with a movie camera and shown in rapid succession to create the movement of the cartoon.

convex – a surface that curves outward, like a rounded bulge.

developer – a chemical used to make the image on exposed film visible.

exposure – a piece of film with an image on it that is made by letting light rays reach the film.

filoscope – a book of photographs, called a flick-book, of a scene or object that moves slightly from one picture to the next. When someone flicked through the pages of the book, the scene or object appeared to be moving.

fixer – a chemical used to set, or make permanent, an image on a developed film exposure.

focal length – the distance from the center of a camera lens to the point where the light rays from a subject in focus come together on the focal plane.

focal plane – the flat area inside and at the back of a camera that holds the camera's film flat and where the light rays meet when the image of the subject is in focus.

hologram – a three-dimensional photograph, made with laser light, in which your view of the subject changes when you move your head from side to side to look at it from different angles.

latent image – an image that has been recorded but does not show up on black-and-white film that has been exposed to light rays that break down the film's light-sensitive crystals. The film must be developed with chemicals before the image becomes visible.

metering system – an electronic light sensor in almost every camera that measures the amount of light coming from a subject or scene and figures out the amount of exposure to the light rays needed for the speed of film being used.

monochrome – one color, like a black-and-white photograph.

panning – moving a camera smoothly in the same direction as your subject moves to prevent the action from being blurred when you actually shoot the picture.

pentaprism – the glass block inside an SLR camera that ensures a clear image, like a reflection in water, without the ghostly second image that appears in a mirror reflection.

phenakistoscope – a popular toy of the nineteenth century that made a series of pictures (similar to those in a filoscope but arranged around the outside of a circle) look like animation when the circle was twirled around.

photomicrograph – a close-up photo taken through a microscope by using the lens of the microscope in place of the normal lens in an SLR camera.

pixel – a tiny dot of color that, together with many other pixels of any of millions of different colors, helps form the digital image of a video display.

polarizing filter – one of several kinds of photographic filters that fits over, or in front of, the camera lens. The polarizing filter lets some, but not all, light rays through the lens specifically to make reflections and strong light disappear in the photo. It also makes the sky look bluer. Other filters are used to correct different lighting problems or produce different effects.

reflection – light rays from an image that bounce off objects with shiny surfaces, like mirrors.

refraction – light rays that may make an image look distorted when seen through glass or water because they have been bent by the glass or water as they pass through.

resolution – the amount of detail that shows in the image of a video display depending on the number of pixels, or dots, into which the image is divided. High-resolution describes sharp, detailed images that have a large number of pixels. Low-resolution describes fuzzy images that do not contain a large number of pixels.

SLR – (single-lens reflex) a type of camera that lets you see exactly what the camera lens sees when you look through the viewfinder.

telephoto doubler – an extension tube that fits between the body and the lens of an SLR camera and doubles the focal length of the lens in order to focus on subjects that are very close up.

transparency – slide or movie film that has a positive rather than a negative image.

BOOKS

Animation. George Parkin (Price Stern Sloan)

Camera. Joan Hewitt (Houghton Mifflin)

Come Look with Me: Discovering Photographs with Children. Jean S. Tucker (Thomasson-Grant)

First Photos: How Kids Can Take Great Pictures. Art Evans (Photo Data Research)

George Eastman. Paul Joseph (Abdo and Daughters)

Light. Science Works (series). Steve Parker (Gareth Stevens)

Machines and Inventions. Record Breakers (series). Peter Lafferty (Gareth Stevens)

My First Photography Book. Dave King (DK Publishing, Inc.)

Photography: Preserving the Past. Bradley Steffens (Lucent Books)

Photography: Take Your Best Shot. Terri Morgan and Shmuel Thaler (Lerner Group)

The Science of Color (series). Barbara J. Behm and Donna Bailey (Gareth Stevens)

Shadow Play: Making Pictures with Light and Lenses. Bernie Zubrowski (Morrow)

Starting Photography. Michael Langford (Butterworth-Heinemann)

VIDEOS

Amy the Photographer. (The Multimedia Co.)

Focus On Photography. (Encyclopædia Britannica Educational Corporation)

Photographer. (New Dimension Media, Inc.)

Photography. (Agency for Instructional Technology)

Photography: A History. (Barr Media Group)

WEB SITES

www.88.com/exposure

www.nh.ultranet.com/~stewoody

Some web sites stay current longer than others. For further web sites, use your search engines to locate the following topics: *animation, cameras, Disney, film, IMAX, movie cameras, photography, and prisms.*

INDEX

PICTURE CREDITS

b=bottom, t=top, c=center, l=left, r=right

Aardman Animations Ltd: p 56br. Mary Evans Picture library: p 4bl; 54br. Galaxy Picture Library: p 61tr. Tim Grabham: p 57tr. Nigel Cattlin/Holt studios international: p 39tl, tr; 55bl; 60bl; 63tl. Robin Kerrod: p 61tl. Microscopix: p 60r. Laurence Gould/Oxford Scientific Films: p 50tr. Chris Oxlade: p 49tr. Papilio Photographic: p 54bl; 63bl, tr, tl. The Projection Box: p 56tl; 58tl. Science Photo Library: Phillipe Plailly p 51bl; Sinclair Stammers 60tl; Francoise Sauze 61bl; George Bernard 61br. Tony Stone Images: p 57br. Lucy Tizard: p 44tl. Zefa Pictures: p 5bl, br; 36bl; 49bl; 50bl; 51t.

j771
Oxlade

40535

Cameras

DATE DUE